£1-20

The Calderstones - a prehistoric tomb in Liverpool

CW00550402

Contents

List of figures

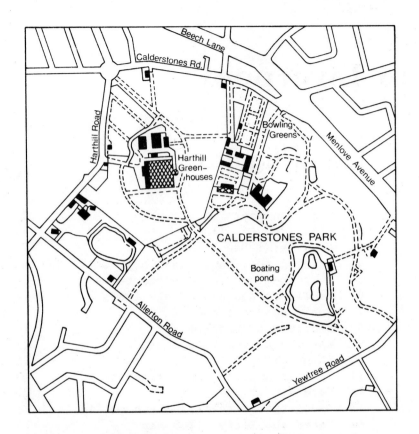

Figure 1   Location of Harthill Greenhouses, Calderstones Park
(Crown Copyright reserved).

Introduction

Over 4,000 years ago, a group of new stone age, or <u>neolithic</u>, farmers built a stone and earthen tomb in what is now Allerton on the outskirts of Liverpool. It is an example of a type of monument that was widespread in the neolithic period throughout large areas of western Europe (fig 5). The tombs were important features in the lives of the earliest farming communities in these regions and are one of the main sources of evidence about them to survive. All that remains of this tomb, however, are six large stones called the Calderstones, moved from their original site and now erected in Harthill Greenhouses, Calderstones Park, Liverpool, (fig 1), where they are available for viewing. Although the tomb itself was destroyed about AD 1833, descriptions from 19th century historians, and the survival of early maps and documents, allows us to understand the meaning behind these stones.

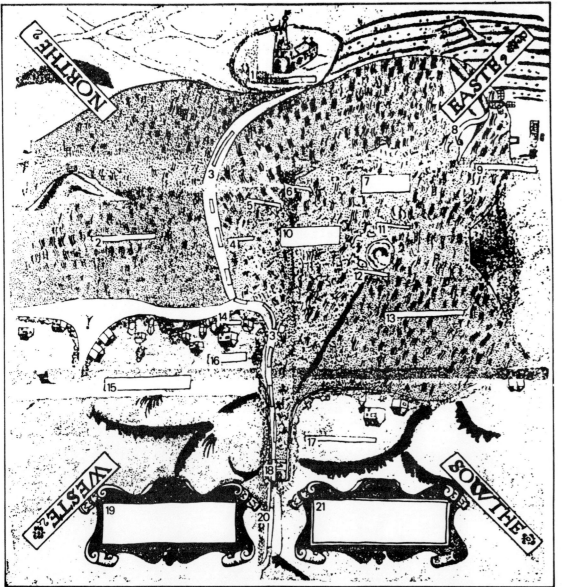

Wavertree claim

1   THE PARISHE churche of Childwall
2   the waste landes belonging to Wauertree
3   the waye that leadeth to the churche of Childwall
4   the little mear
5   the crosse yatte
14 Pembertons yatte
15 Ye seuerall landes of our moste Gracious souerayne
    lady ye Quene within herr manner of wauertree 19
16 Pembertons howsse
19 In this table is mensioned howe the meares and
    boundaries Aledged for our soueraigne lady the Quene
    Doo lye and bounde And what distaunce they bee one fro
    Another. Fyrst beginninge at a yatte in thend of
    Bowells lane and so folloinge Northest to ye corner of
    the hedge of the seuerall landes of henry mossocke
    beinge distante frome the sayde yatte Twenty & seuen
    roodes. Frome the sayde corner goinge est by north unto
    A stone standinge on ye south weste side pykelohill &
    ffyuescore foure roodes. Frome the sayde stone Northest
    to another stone standinge on the northest side of the
    sayde pykeloohill fowre roodes. From that stone est by
    northe to another stone called Rodgerstone sixtene
    roodes. From that stone Est northest to three stones
    called Calldway stones fortye fyue roodes & a halfe.

Allerton claim

6   ye mickle mear
7   ye calledway stones called by ye quenes tenantes
    And called bye ye tenantes of Richerd Lathame the
    doferstones otherwise Rogerstones or calldway
    stones
8   ye winde milne A Allerton
9   the hall of Allartonn
10 This is ye lande in variance betwene ye Quenes
    tenants of herr manner of Wauertree And Ric.
    Lathame esquyer Lorde of Allartonn whiche sayde
    landes dote amounte to ye quantite of 39 Accers &
    two falls. A great measure accomptinge eight yerdes
    to the roode.
11 The Rodgerstone
12 The pykeloohill
13 The waste landes belonging to Allerton
17 Ye seuerall landes of henry mossocke
18 Bowells lane
21 In this table is mensioned howe the meares and
    boundaries Alledged for Ric[d] Lathame esquyer doo lye &
    bounde & what distaunce they bee one from another.
    Fyrst beginninge at ye haregrene diche in thends of
    Bowells lane and so folloinge the quenes seuerall
    landes northest unto the uppemost corner y[e]rof near
    pembertons howsse beinge distant frome the same
    fourescore seuen roods. From the sayde corner folloinge
    the highe way northwest A yatte Anenst pembertons
    howsse Twelve roods. From the sayde yatte northest to
    ye little mear fforty eight roodes. Frome y[e] sayde mear
    est to ye crosse gatte. Twenty fowre roodes. From ye
    sayde crosse gatte est by south to ye Mickle mear nine
    tene roods. From ye sayde mickle mear southest by est
    unto three stones called Dojer stones other wyse Rodge
    stones or Calldway stones fforty seuen roods & a halfe

4 Figure 2   Plan made in the 1568 boundary dispute between Allerton
        and Wavertree (redrawn).

How do we know the Calderstones were part of a tomb?

The Calderstones were first referred to as 'the dojer, rojer or Caldwaye stones' in a boundary dispute between Wavertree and Allerton in 1568. The accompanying map (fig 2) shows three stones set in a roughly oval mound. We also learn from a witness in the dispute, Robert Mercer of West Derby, that a fourth stone had been removed about 18 years previously. The mound was subsequently disturbed several times until it was finally destroyed about AD 1833, (see p 25). A letter of the time, quoting a young farmhand who remembered the act, states that when '...the stones were dug down to...They looked as if they had been a little hut or cellar. Below the stones was found a large quantity of burnt bones, white and in small pieces. He thought there must have been a cartload or two.'

Large stones forming a cellar-like chamber, beneath a circular mound, and with quantities of burnt bone, are all features assoc-iated with surviving communal tombs of the neolithic period. The stones in the Harthill Greenhouses also have remarkable carvings on them, some very similar to those on known neolithic tombs found throughout Europe, but particularly to those found in Ireland and north Wales in the later neolithic period.

What did these tombs look like?

The tombs of which the Calderstones is an example are often
called megalithic from the Greek words 'megas' meaning 'great' and
'lithos' meaning 'stone'. They are also referred to as chambered tombs.
Tombs of this type found in Britain were built from about 3,500 bc
until about 2,000 bc. Tombs found in the Boyne valley in Ireland have
carvings most similar to those on the Calderstones; they date from late
in this time span, from about 2,500 bc, or later, and are of a
particular type known as passage graves.

In passage graves the central stone chamber can be formed
either by several large upright stones set on edge, when they are known
as orthostats, or by a dry stone walling technique, or a combination of
both. The stone chambers may be either circular or polygonal, or have
small lateral extensions to the basic design giving a cruciform plan.
The chambers are roofed by either a single large flat slab, known as a
capstone, resting on the walls, or by a technique of overlapping small
stones, known as corbelling. The chambers may vary in width and height
between 1 and 7 metres.

Earthen mounds, almost exclusively circular, are set over the
chambers. These range from about 15 metres in diameter, to about 90
metres at tombs such as New Grange in the Boyne Valley in Ireland. A
stone-lined passage of either orthostatic or dry-walled construction
leads from the outside through the mound to the chamber. Occasionally
the mound itself is surrounded or revetted by a circle of orthostats.

There is no surviving evidence that the Calderstones tomb ever
included a passage. However markings similar to those on the stones,
when found on other tombs, are almost always associated with passage
graves. It is likely therefore that the Calderstones did originally
include a stone-lined passage. The small number of stones found when
the mound was destroyed implies that those originally flanking such a
passage must have been missing by the late 19th century. That three of

Figure 3   The passage grave at Bryn Celli Ddu.

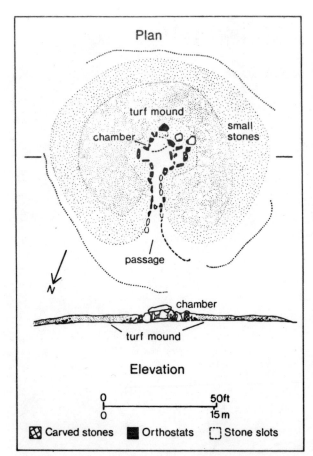

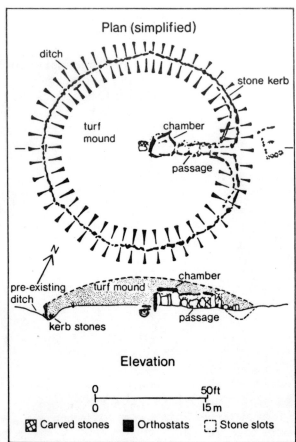

Figure 4   Barclodiad y Gawres (left) and Bryn Celli Ddu (right)
(after Lynch, 1969).

the six stones forming the chamber were visible in 1568 could be
explained by the partial collapse of the mound over the chamber. This
may have occured after the tomb had ceased to be used for burials when
the more accessible stones lining the passage were robbed for use else-
where.

The two nearest tombs to the Calderstones are on Anglesey, at
Barclodiad y Gawres and Bryn Celli Ddu, both passage graves,
(fig 4). The former possesses carvings similar to those on Irish graves
and the Calderstones, and has a tomb plan comparable to many Irish
examples. In western Britain and Ireland there are several different
styles of tomb design, each one restricted to fairly distinct
geographical areas. It is therefore to the Boyne Valley and north
Wales, and particularly to the nearer Welsh examples that we should
most probably turn to get some idea of what the Calderstones may have
looked like. What follows, however, can only be a general guide, as the
Calderstones are likely to have differed in some aspects.

The tomb at Barclodiad y Gawres has a passage about 7 metres
long leading to a cruciform chamber under a circular 30 metre diameter
mound. Bryn Celli Ddu has a passage 1 metre wide and 9 metres long,
leading to a simpler polygonal chamber 2 to 3 metres across, beneath a
mound similarly about 30 metres in diameter. A circle of standing
stones, laid in the ditch of an earlier monument on the site, surrounds
this tomb. This tomb has features which link it with Brittany as much
as with Ireland. The discovery of a 'hut or cellar' when the
Calderstones' mound was destroyed suggests that it may have contained
the simpler form of chamber. This is reinforced by the fact that only
six large stones were recovered.

Who built the tombs?

Most excavated chambered tombs have been found to contain the bones of many individuals, often dispersed in disorder across the burial chamber. In the Calderstones 'several cartloads' of bones were found. Finds from many other tombs also suggest that they were kept in use for long periods, often hundreds of years, before finally being blocked up. This collective form of burial, therefore, appears to have been a continuous process with older burials making way for new ones within the tombs. The people who were buried in them may have belonged to generations of the same family-linked groups who probably formed the basic social or tribal groupings in neolithic society.

Evidence from other parts of Britain shows that these small groups lived by herding domesticated animals and growing cereals, although at present we have no evidence for cereal farming in the neolithic in this part of north-west England. It seems likely that neolithic agriculture was based on a shifting pattern. Small clearings made in the woodlands would be farmed for a number of years until the soil became exhausted. The group would then move on to make new clearings and settlements nearby. The tombs may, therefore, also have acted as symbols of identity, and as territorial markers for these social groups.

As with other tombs of this kind, the Calderstones may still have been in use in the early bronze age period, about 4,000 years ago. The markings of apparently different dates on some of the stones (p 20) could only have been carved if the tomb remained open a long time. There is also some evidence that bronze age people used the tomb for their own burial rites. The several references in the 19th century literature about the Calderstones, to a 'sepulchral urn, rudely ornamented outside' and 'urns made of the coarsest clay, containing human dust and bones' suggest the bronze age tradition of cremated burials in pottery urns. Several other megalithic tombs bear witness to the practise of inserting bronze age cremation urns into the mounds of earlier neolithic tombs.

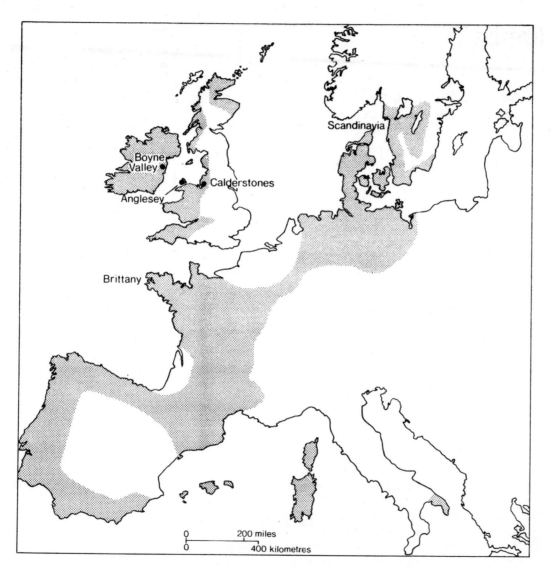

Figure 5   The distribution of neolithic chambered tombs in
western Europe (after Renfrew, 1973).

11

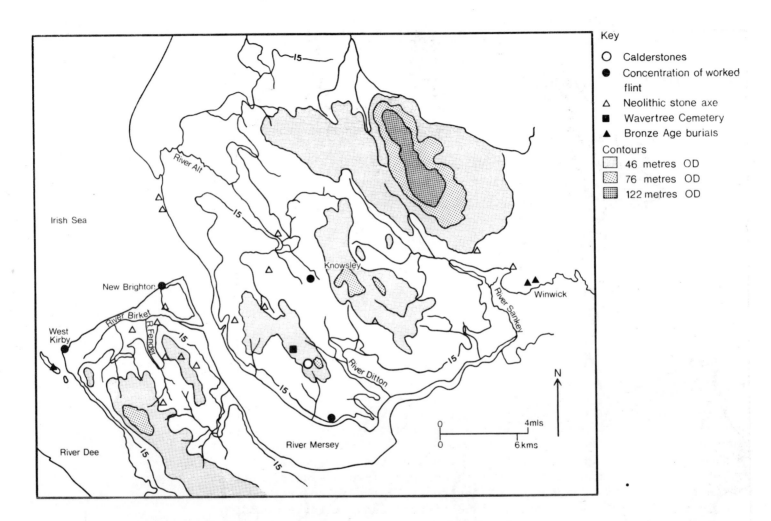

Key

O Calderstones
● Concentration of worked
   flint
△ Neolithic stone axe
■ Wavertree Cemetery
▲ Bronze Age burials

Contours

☐ 46 metres OD
▨ 76 metres OD
▧ 122 metres OD

Figure 6   Evidence of neolithic and bronze age activity in the
            Merseyside area.

What did the area look like in prehistoric times?

      Much of south-west Lancashire consists of large, flat areas of boulder clay mixed with expanses of sand and peat. In the neolithic period much of this was covered by heavy woodland on ill-drained soils, and by bogs or lakes. By contrast the area of Allerton, in which the tomb stood, is an elevated area of sand-stone producing lighter, better drained soils. The natural wooded vegetation would have been more easily cleared here and would, therefore, have been more attractive for settlement and farming throughout the prehistoric period. Early maps and documents show that the tomb was originally located at the head of a small valley leading from the sandstone plateau on to the boulder clay, near to the edge of the present bowling greens (fig 1).

      Where the people who used the Calderstones lived is, however, not known, but the main archaeological evidence for the immediate area is shown in figure 6. Small concentrations of stone tools found near the rivers Mersey and Alt and at New Brighton on the Wirral coast may mark settlement sites of some kind, and there is evidence that late neolithic man may have been clearing woodland to the north-east of the Alt, in the district of Knowsley. Several neolithic stone axeheads have also been found scattered across the region. Axeheads were important items of exchange, and probably represent the existence of trade routes in the area coupled with the clearance of woodland.

      There may also have been a second burial tomb several hundred metres to the south-west of the Calderstones, although no written records of it survive. The map of 1568 (fig 2) shows a large mound,

13

known as Pykloo or Pykelaw Hill flanked by two upright stones about 30 metres apart. A third standing stone lay between the mound and the Calderstones. It seems possible that this mound was either neolithic or bronze age in date. Passage graves, both in Britain and Europe are often grouped together in cemeteries.

A further possibly connected feature in the area is the standing stone known as Robin Hood's Stone (fig 7) now situated at the junction of Booker Avenue and Archerfield Road. This stone has vertical grooves on its upper part, similar to those on one of the Calderstones, which may be natural. At one time the grooves were explained as marks caused by sharpening arrows in the medieval period. A more fanciful idea in the 19th century was that they were grooves for draining the blood of sacrificial victims of the Druids!

It seems likely that the stone was in some way linked with the prehistoric burial or ritual practices of the area. An early photograph of the stone shows that on the end now lying beneath the ground surface, are what appear to be several cup marks, generally thought to be bronze age in date (p 20). The Robin Hood Stone may always have been an isolated standing stone, or it may have been moved at a much later date from the Calderstones, or from its immediate vicinity. It may possibly be the stone referred to as having been removed from the mound about 1550.

That the area remained a focus for settlement into the bronze age, is suggested by the secondary burials in the Calderstones mound, and is also shown by the discovery in 1867 of a now demolished bronze age flat cemetery containing 8 cremation urns, which was situated about 1½ miles to the north, in Wavertree. Two of these urns (fig 9) are now in Merseyside County Museums, Liverpool. Other urns were found near West Kirby on Wirral in the 19th century. In 1980 three urns and three accessory vessels were excavated from beneath a burial mound just on Merseyside's border at Winwick. Radiocarbon dates indicate two phases of use of the mound between about 1,700 bc and 1,400 bc.

Figure 7   Robin Hood's Stone (redrawn after photograph in
            Stewart-Brown, 1925).

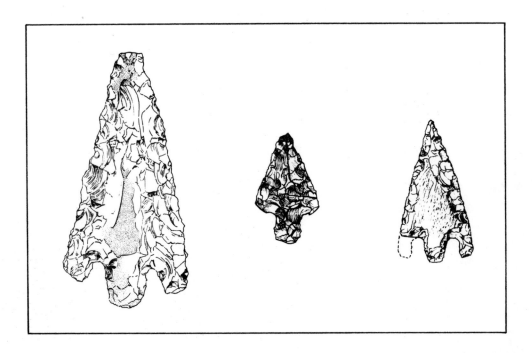

Figure 8   Early bronze age arrowheads from the Calderstones area.

Large parts of Merseyside were still heavily wooded during the bronze age, and finds of distinctive <u>barbed</u> <u>and</u> <u>tanged</u> arrowheads of this period (fig 8) have been made, suggesting wide-ranging hunting of wild animals in the area. Three such arrowheads have been found from within a mile of the Calderstones.

Figure 9   Cremation urns from the bronze age cemetery in
            Wavertree (photo courtesy of Merseyside County
            Museums).

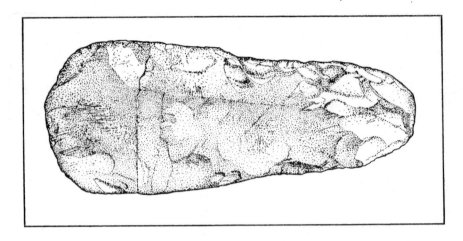

Figure 10   Stone axe from Parliament Field, Toxteth.

The carvings on the Calderstones

There are six main categories of markings on the stones: (i)
spirals, either single, conjoined or arranged as a face motif;
(ii) concentric circles; (iii) arcs; (iv) small circular depressions in
the rock known as cup marks; (v) cup marks in association with circles
known as cup and ring marks; and (vi) footprints.

Spirals are found carved on many tombs in Ireland,
particularly on those forming the large late neolithic cemetery
in the Boyne Valley. Parallels are also found on two tombs in Anglesey
at Barclodiad y Gawres and at Bryn Celli Ddu. The Irish examples and
those at Barclodiad y Gawres are however more complex than the spirals
found on the Calderstones (fig 11). Conjoined spirals, as in C4, C5

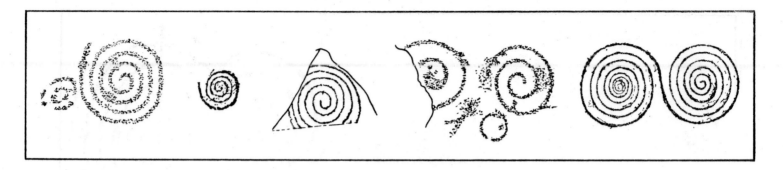

Figure 11   Examples of 'passage grave' art: (left to right)
             Spirals from the Calderstones, Dowth (Ireland) and
             Barclodiad y Gawres (Wales). Conjoined spirals from the
             Calderstones and New Grange (Ireland).

and C5a and the associated face motifs B5, C6 and E9 are also common
types in Irish art, as are the concentric circles which are found on
five stones at Calderstones. The sun or wheel motif is also very
common on tombs in the Boyne Valley. All these similarities imply that
cultural influences were being brought into this region from Ireland,
probably via north Wales, around 2,000 bc.
        The combined straight line and concentric circle design of A1
(fig 17), however, is quite individual although there are designs found
on Irish and Welsh graves that could have inspired the motif. The
doubled back outer line in spiral E8 (fig 21) is peculiar to this tomb
and might also be seen as a local development. These signs of local
development are possibly a reflection on the geographical isolation of
the Calderstones from the main centre of art inspiration in Ireland.
        The footprint motifs are more difficult to date. They are found at
three sites in Ireland, six in Scotland, and at one in England, and
except at the latter, are not associated with megalithic tombs. Nor are

19

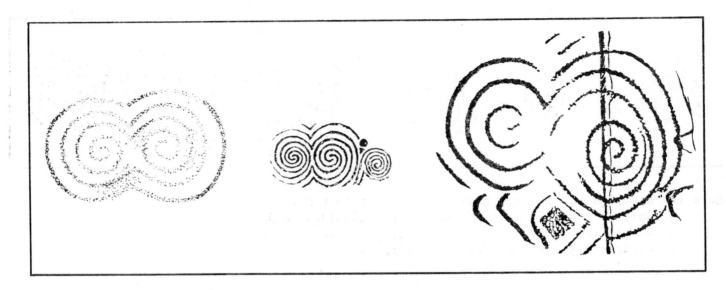

Figure 12 Examples of 'passage grave' art: (left to right) Face
motifs from the Calderstones, New Grange (Ireland) and
Barclodiad y Gawres (Wales).

the footmarks similar in style. These kinds of markings are of a type
not commonly associated with neolithic tombs. They, and the cup and
ring marks found on some of the Calderstones, are possibly of early
bronze age date. Motif B9 (fig 18), the halberd, is also assumed to be
of this period. Given the length of time tombs of this type could
remain open, bronze age markings on the stones are quite likely.

Footmarks are found widespread in Scandinavia, although only one
example is on a tomb, but there are few stylistic similarities. They
are also found in Brittany, although again only once on a tomb. This is
called the Dolmen du Petit Mont, and the examples from there have the
closest stylistic links with those on the Calderstones, although the
method of carving is more sophisticated.

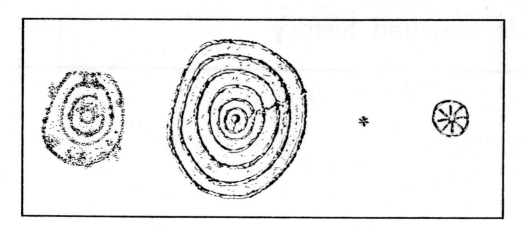

Figure 13 Examples of 'passage grave' art: (left to right)
          Concentric circles from the Calderstones and Knockamany
          (Ireland). Sun or wheel motifs from the Calderstones
          and Loughcrew (Ireland).

        Other markings on the stones, the bootprints on stone D
(fig 20), the cross on B11 (fig 18) and possibly the Maltese cross E3
(fig 21) are all much later and date from after the stones were exposed
by the erosion or destruction of the covering mound. In recent years a
number of modern grafitti have also been carved on the stones.
        The Calderstones can, therefore, be seen from the similarities
present in the carvings to be closely but not exclusively associated
with Ireland and Wales. Cultural influences were arriving from the
south west sea route as well, particularly from Brittany. The river
Mersey must have played an important part both in the initial
settlement of this area in the neolithic period and in the continuing
cultural links between widely dispersed groups of people.

Calderstones — documented history

Date	Documentary evidence	Comments
c1550	One stone removed.	
1568	Boundary point on drawn plan; the three stones are called 'dojer stones otherwyse Rodger stones or Calldway stones'.	Stones shown on a mound.
1700	Boundary dispute; describes three stones set on a little ascent or rising ground called 'Dogger Stones or Caldway Stones'.	
c1765	Report of the mound being disturbed by 'digging about them (the stones); urn containing 'human dust and bones' found. Another report of roughly the same date says 'several' cinerary urns had been found.	Probably bronze age secondary interments ie after the first phase of use of the tomb had ended.
1768	Map of area by Yates and Perry (fig 14).	The first published plan showing the location of the Calderstones.
pre-1805	'High and extensive mound on which stones formerly stood' largely destroyed to provide sand for making mortar when Bragg's house on Woolton Road was built. Report of another urn being found in the debris.	

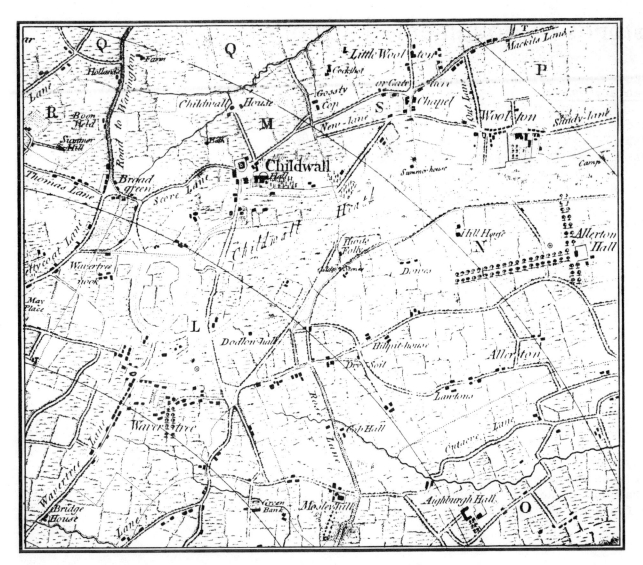

Figure 14   Detail of 'Map of the Environs of Liverpool' (1768) by
Yates and Perry, showing the Calderstones.

23

Figure 15   The Calderstones, drawn in 1825.

Date	Documentary evidence	Comments
c1833	The mound finally destroyed when the road was widened; 'little hut or cellar' formed by stones, a cart-load or two of burnt bones also found, no artefacts reported. The stones were laid aside on a farm, some were later set up in a circle near their original site at the roadside by the entrance to the Park. One is reported as having been taken by a Mr Booker and set up as a rubbing stone for his cattle, reportedly the Robin Hood stone.	But on a map of 1772 the former field where the stone stood was already called Stone Hey, suggesting it was placed there before 1772.
1845	By this date the stones had been arranged in a circle and enclosed by a low stone wall by Mr Need-Walker.	The wall still exists at the entrance to the Park.
1954	Stones removed to Calderstones Park by City Corporation.	
1964	Stones redisplayed in vestibule to Harthill Greenhouses.	

25

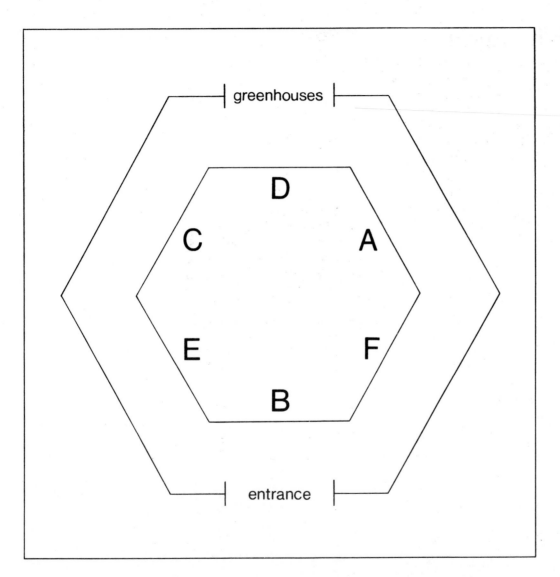

Figure 16   The arrangement of the Calderstones in Harthill
            Greenhouses, Calderstones Park.

The Stones — a guide

The stones were moved to their present location in 1964, and placed in random order as you see them now. They are of local sandstone which outcrops widely in the vicinity. On them have been carved a number of motifs which are paralleled on other chambered tombs. The motifs have mainly been executed by a pecking of the surface rather than by gouging.

Long periods of atmospheric weathering have meant that many of the carvings are now all but invisible. In 1954, when they were removed from their earlier site just outside the gates of the Park, they were covered with a black patina or film as well as by growth of moss. When the stones were cleaned, latex moulds were made of the carvings which have preserved an accurate record of them and helped to show up some very worn motifs which were not previously visible.

In the following pages all markings existing on the stones have been shown, but those that cannot be clearly seen are numbered in brackets. Each stone has been given a letter, and each motif on that stone a number, for ease of identification. The numbering system is that used in the publication by Forde-Johnston who was originally responsible for recording and cleaning the stones (see Further Reading).

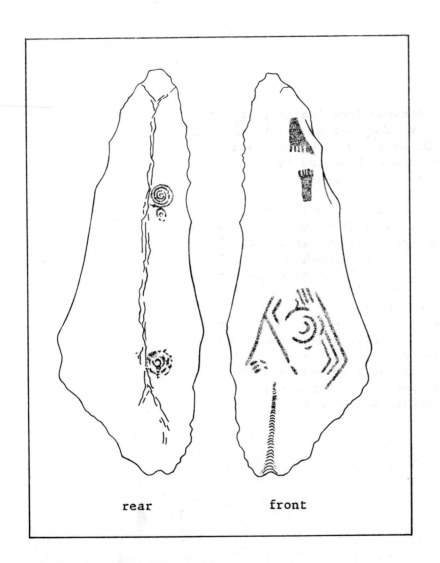

rear   front

Figure 17   Stone A.

28

Stone A

A little over 2.5 metres in height and about 1 metre in width, the lower part of the front face is covered by a black patina.

Front face

A1   This motif consists of 3 central concentric circles slightly overlapping a series of parallel lines to each side, with inward turns above and below. A curved line leads towards part of another vague circular motif. Only part of the outer concentric circle of the main circular motif is clearly visible.

A4   Footmark with deeply cut squared heel clearly defined.

A5   Larger footmark, less clearly defined but still visible.

Rear face

A2   Spiral of four and a quarter turns, clearly visible.

A2a   Two concentric circles of slightly loose form; visible though not clearly defined.

(A3) Spiral similar to A2 although more irregular in shape; very badly eroded and not visible to the naked eye.

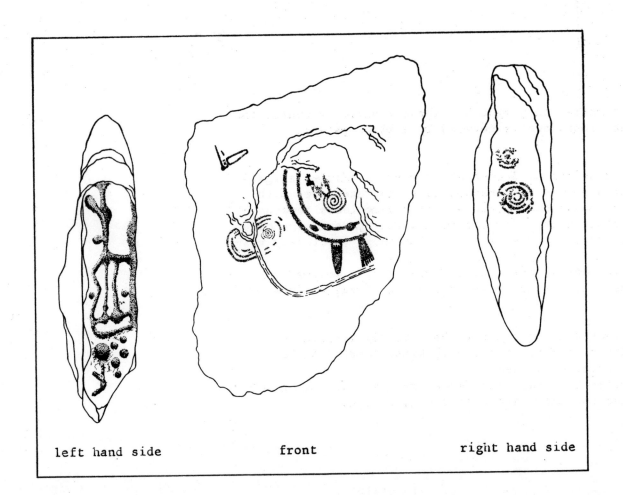

left hand side   front   right hand side

Figure 18 Stone B.

Stone B

About 2 metres long and 1.5 metres wide with a maximum thickness
of about 0.5 metres. There are markings on only one face and two
edges. Some parts of the surface appear to have been lost due to
the flaking off of the sandstone.

Front face

B2   A regular three and two-thirds spiral, much worn.

B3   Two arcs, possibly reduced in length by breaking off of
stone; visible.

B5   Incomplete face motif with traces of concentric circles in
centre, deep groove in the rock divides the motif down the
middle. Only outer arc markings are plain but even these are
not clearly visible.

B6   Footprint with 6 toes, joined to arc B3; visible.

(B7) Footprint joined to arc B3 by the toes; not clearly visible.

(B8) Incomplete footmark, heel of which partially overlaps outer
part of spiral B2; is itself overlain by B11; not clearly
visible.

B9   Possibly a halberd (a type of bronze age axe), the vertical
line representing the haft; clearly visible.

(B11) Overlapping the footmark B8 is the heel of another foot; is
itself overlain by a much later cross; not clearly visible.

Right hand side

B1   Group of 4 concentric circles; clearly visible.

(B4) Either a spiral or group of concentric circles; very worn,
not clearly visible.

Left hand side

B10   Combination of interlinked grooved and circular cupmarks.

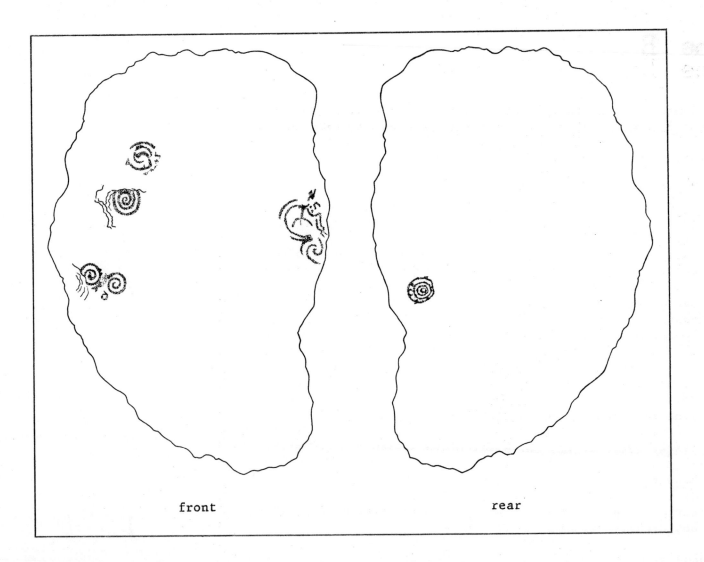

front   rear

Figure 19 Stone C.

Stone C

The largest, nearly 3 metres long and 2 metres wide, 0.27 metres
thick. The edges of the stone at C6 may have been broken away.

Front face

C2   Spiral; of two and a half turns; motif weathered but clearly
       visible.

C3   Incomplete spiral, probably 3 turns. Weathered, although
       still clear markings on outer edges; clearly visible.

(C4)   Incomplete two and a half turns spiral.

(C5a) Small circle attached to what may be the outer end of a
       spiral.

The last three motifs appear to be linked, the whole composition
forming a face motif; not clearly visible.

(C6)   Very badly eroded, but latex mould impressions suggest
       another face motif, weakly delineated to the lower right and
       overlain by indistinct motif to the upper right; not clearly
       visible.

Rear face

C1   Group of 4 concentric circles; clearly visible.

On both faces are numerous cup marks which are not shown in the
illustrations.

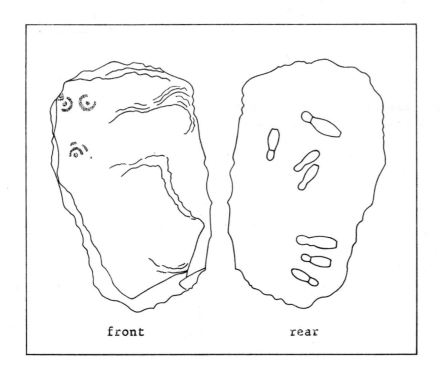

front   rear

Figure 20   Stone D.

Stone D

About 3 metres long and 1 metre wide.

Front face
(D1) Cup and ring mark, ring incomplete, merges into triangle
      motif; not clearly visible.
D2   Cup and ring mark, ring almost complete; clearly visible.
(D3) Cup mark with 2 rings, inner ring more complete; not clearly
      visible.

Rear face
7 outlines of boots, executed in the 19th century.

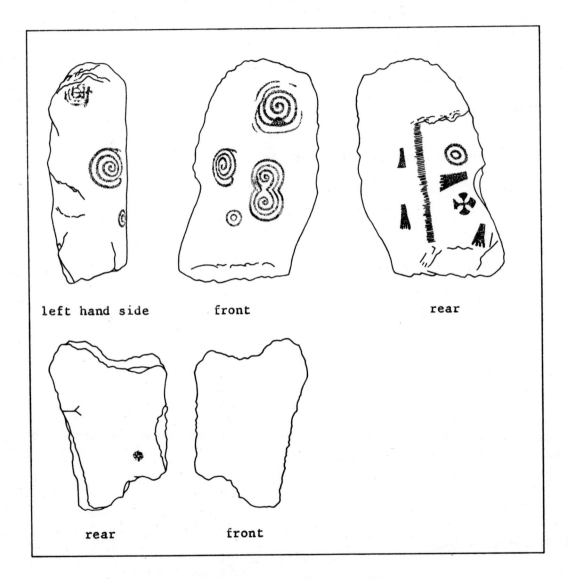

left hand side   front   rear

rear   front

Figure 21 Stone E (above) and Stone F (below).

Stone E

1.5 metres long, 1 metre wide and about 0.60 metres thick.

Front face

E7   3 full turns spiral, well defined, surrounded by narrow and shallower lines forming 2 more incomplete turns; clearly visible.

E8   On the curved surface is another circle, $2\frac{3}{4}$ anti-clockwise turns with a full turn in the opposite direction; clearly visible though shaded by ferns.

(E9)   Badly weathered double conjoined spirals or face motif with figure of eight appearence; not clearly visible.

(E10) 2 small concentric circles.

(E11) Irregular badly worn spiral, only two and one third turns clear; not clearly visible.

Rear face

E1   2 concentric circles; clearly visible.

E2   Footprint, squared heel with prominent big toe; clearly visible.

E3   Maltese cross, generally attributed to the medieval period; partly hidden beneath ground level.

(E4)   Footmark with only 4 toes; beneath ground level.

E5   Footmark with squared heel; clearly visible.

(E6)   Probable footmark without toes; not clearly visible.

Stone F

About 1 metre long and 0.75 metres wide.

Rear face

F1   Sun or wheel motif.

Glossary

barbed and tanged arrowhead
: a type of flint arrowhead with a central projection opposite the point, known as the tang, which fastened to the arrow shaft, on either side of which is a further projection, the barb.

capstone
: a stone slab resting on the upright walls of a burial chamber made of stone.

chambered tomb
: a burial mound of long, round or other form which contains a burial chamber made of stone.

corbelling
: a method of roofing a stone chamber by laying successive courses of small stone slabs on the chamber wall with each course inwardly overlapping the course below. The final gap can be bridged by a single capstone. This method produces a rough dome-like appearance.

cruciform
: a form of stone chamber produced by adding small chambers either side of and at right angles to the central chamber, giving a plan resembling a cross.

cup marks
: simple, roughly circular depressions carved in the stone. They occur not only on some chambered tombs but also on standing stones, stone circles and natural boulders.

cup and ring mark
: a cup mark with encircling carved ring.

dry stone walling
: laying small stones on top of each other without any bonding material.

flat cemetery
: a group of burials, either inhumations or cremations in pottery vessels, not covered by earthen or stone mounds, particularly associated with the earlier bronze age.

halberd	a dagger-like bronze implement, found in bronze age contexts.
megalithic	a form of construction using large stones.
neolithic	the period of the first farming communities, in Britain dating from about 3,500 bc to 2,000 bc.
orthostat	a large stone slab. When several are laid on edge in the ground next to one another to form a structure, it is said to be of orthostatic construction.
passage grave	a grave consisting of a narrow stone-lined passage leading to a higher and wider stone burial chamber.
radio carbon	a method of dating dead organic material, such as charcoal, peat, bone etc by scientifically measuring the amount of radioactive carbon left in a sample. The dates are given in radio carbon years (bc). Certain adjustments (calibration) have to be made to these dates to allow for known inaccuracies in the method. The revised or calibrated dates are always earlier by several hundred years and are given as BC, ie calendar years. Because a universally accepted calibration is not yet in force, radio carbon years are used in this report.
revetted	a mound of earth or stone surrounded and held in place by a ring of stones set on edge.

Further reading

G Coffey	1977	New Grange and other Incised Tumuli in Ireland. Dolphin Press.
G E Daniel	1950	The Prehistoric Chamber Tombs of England and Wales. Cambridge.
	1958	The Megalithic Builders of Western Europe. Hutchinson University Library.
J L Forde-Johnston	1956	"The Calderstones, Liverpool", reprinted from Barclodiad y Gawres by T G E Powell and G E Daniel. Liverpool University Press.
	1957	"Megalithic Art in the North West of Britain, the Calderstones, Liverpool" Proceedings of the Prehistoric Society vol. 23, 20-39.
R W B Morris	1979	The Prehistoric Rock Art of Galloway and the Isle of Man. Blandford Press.
T G E Powell (ed.)	1969	Megalithic Enquiries in the West of Britain. Liverpool University Press.
A C Renfrew	1973	Before Civilisation. Penguin.
(ed.)	1981	The Megalithic Monuments of Western Europe. Thames and Hudson.
R Stewart-Brown	1911	A History of the Manor and Township of Allerton. Liverpool.